How to Relate to Parents After Your Marriage

Honoring Them While Loving Your Spouse

Chris Polski

New Growth Press
newgrowthpress.com

New Growth Press, Greensboro, NC 27401
newgrowthpress.com

Cover Design: Dan Stelzer
Interior Typesetting and Ebook: Lisa Parnell,
lparnellbookservices.com

ISBN: 978-1-64507-641-4 (paperback)
ISBN: 978-1-64507-642-1 (ebook)

Library of Congress Cataloging-in-Publication Data on file

Printed in India

30 29 28 27 26 1 2 3 4 5

Honor your father and your mother,
that your days may be long in the land
that the LORD *your God is giving you.*
—Exodus 20:12

Once the whirlwind of our honeymoon had died down and we'd set up our home, established our schedules, and figured out what "normal" life looked like as a married couple, my wife and I soon faced our first big decision: Where would we spend our first Christmas together?

We had enough on our plate trying to put together a new house, sorting out our weekly life rhythms, and trying not to get in each other's way in our tiny bathroom. But once our parents posed the question, we realized we were going to have to figure something out.

My wife's parents lived in the same town as we did, so we saw them quite often. My parents, on the other hand, lived in Florida, which meant that we didn't get to see them as much. But that wasn't the only factor in play. There was also a significant difference in the way our two families celebrated Christmas.

My wife's family had big Christmas traditions with lots of extended family members in town, accompanied by a correspondingly huge (I mean HUGE) pile of presents. They decorated extravagantly and treated Christmas like a weeklong festival with organized family activities and traditions that were years in the making. This meant that they placed an outsized emphasis on gathering the whole family for Christmas. Since we lived in the same town as my wife's family, my own parents, whose traditions weren't as robust, were really hoping that we would visit them—which would mean missing part of the big celebration at my in-laws'—so that they could share in the joy of our first Christmas as a married couple.

We were both highly aware of the complexities of the situation, but neither of us knew how to even begin the conversation about how we would decide what to do. On the one hand, I didn't want to disappoint my own family with a deflected Christmas invitation on our first married Christmas. On the other hand, my wife didn't want to be the one to pour cold water on her own family's traditions by suggesting that there was even a slight chance we might not be home for their celebrations. The whole conversation put us both on edge and threatened to break out into an argument almost every time we tried to discuss it.

What were we going to do? What would *you* do?

If you are a recent newlywed reading this, you can probably relate to grappling with the tricky dynamics that are part of establishing your new family. Not only do you and your spouse each have your own viewpoints about traditions, family time, and your new normal as a married couple, but your families likely have their own opinions too. You might also be wondering what in the world you are supposed to do, especially if your spouse's viewpoint is different from your parents', or even from your own. What does it look like to uphold your commitment to love your spouse while trying simultaneously to honor your own father and mother?

The truth is that this dual calling can be challenging, which means that you (and your parents) are bound to make mistakes. However, there are some wise biblical principles that can help us sort out this common but complex dilemma.

Honoring Your Parents While Loving Your Spouse

One principle that needs to be affirmed up front is that once you are married, your spouse becomes your highest priority, second only to God himself (Genesis 2:24). You've been instructed by God to *leave* your family of origin and *cleave* to your spouse in such a way that you become *one flesh*. This is the essence of Christian marriage. When you follow through on these principles, you transfer your fundamental loyalty away from your parents to your spouse.

But this time of great joy when you unite yourself to your spouse is exactly the moment when you begin to realize that the people who nurtured and sacrificed for you are no longer the principal relationship in your life. Making this change in priority can feel like betraying your parents. You deeply desire to love your spouse but, in most cases, you can't stand the thought of disappointing your parents.

What does the Bible teach us about how we maintain a loving and respectful relationship with our parents after we get married?

Here are three foundational biblical principles that can help us as we consider this important question.

1. Move from obedience to honor

All children have one permanent and one temporary duty to their parents. The permanent call is to *honor* them (more on that in a moment), while the temporary call is to *obey* them.

The temporary duty of obedience is described in Ephesians 6:1–3, where the apostle Paul says,

> Children, obey your parents in the Lord, for this is right. "Honor your father and mother" (this is the first commandment with a promise), "that it may go well with you and that you may live long in the land."

This means that as children living in our parents' home and under their authority, we must do our very best to adhere to their guidelines and expectations (provided they are biblically ethical). But once we've exited their home and come out from under their authority as adults, our duty to obey our parents is removed, leaving us to settle back into our more permanent and abiding duty of *honoring* them.

It doesn't take a rocket scientist to see that this is a terribly difficult transition for parents and their adult children, perhaps even more so when those children are newly married. Parents, who have (usually) poured everything they have into teaching, guiding, and providing for their children, suddenly have a dramatically shifted role in their grown children's lives, and young adults now have to learn what it means to make decisions for themselves.

There are two fundamental dilemmas to consider as you embark on this newlywed journey and establish new parameters in your relationship with your parents. The first is the obvious mathematical fact that when you get married, you usually gain at least two new parents. That means that you are now called to honor *additional* parents, not just two. That's twice as complicated as your situation before marriage. The good news is that your parents probably had to deal with the same thing when they married, which means that they should, at least in principle, be aware from their own life experience of the new dynamics you are facing.

The second dilemma is that old habits die hard. Parents are accustomed to telling their children to do things, and children are likewise used to being told what to do. Many young marriages go off the rails right away because one of the spouse's parents haven't yet made this adjustment and exert significant pressure upon their child to meet their expectations. This can impinge upon the essential bond of marriage.

Unlike our relationship with God, whom we are called to obey for our entire lives, our relationship with our parents changes once we are full-fledged adults. In fact, continuing to be subject to our parents' authority after we've left their home is unbiblical. Scripture teaches us that instead of giving perpetual obedience to your parents, you are called instead to offer continual honor (Exodus 20:12).

In the fifth commandment, the Hebrew word for *honor* is *ka-bad,* and when used in its imperative sense, it means *to glorify* or *make something weighty.*[1] It's a word used most often to describe one of our fundamental duties toward God: celebrating his attributes and virtues. Similarly, we are to aim for a disposition toward our parents that esteems them, considers their wise counsel, and treats them with respect.

The basic idea here is that all children, no matter what their age, are called to celebrate the virtues of their parents. Likewise, they are to carefully consider the wishes of their parents, but only so long as those wishes do not place an inordinate burden on the new marriage that would detract from their primary relationship with their spouse.

An example of an inordinate burden parents might place on a couple is asking them to quit their jobs and uproot their lives to live in the same town as the parents. While perhaps grounded in an understandable desire to be near family, a request like this is not something you should feel pressured to comply with unless you and your spouse see the wisdom in it and desire this change yourselves. An example of a reasonable request from parents is their invitation for you to join them for a big anniversary celebration with plenty of advance notice to work out the logistics.

I should pause here to acknowledge that not everyone's parents have lived in a way that is honorable. Some have been unkind, neglectful, or even abusive. We have a God who understands what it's like to be subject to harsh treatment (Hebrews 2:17–18), and he certainly isn't expecting us to honor anything sinful in our parents' legacies. But there may still be ways of honoring parents who have failed us in some significant way. In cases of abuse, a counselor can help us work through what appropriate and healthy honor might look like. The idea is that Lord wants us to prayerfully wrestle with how we pursue honoring our parents even in less than ideal circumstances. Why? Because when we truly understand the impact of the gospel in our lives and how undeserving we are of God's grace and forgiveness, it will prompt us to look for ways to extend that same grace to those who have wronged us.

2. Move from dependence to responsibility

As we get older, we become more mature. We stop doing the childish things we did when we were kids, and we start taking on the responsibilities of adulthood. This is such a basic truth about growing up that Paul uses it to illustrate harder-to-understand spiritual truths in 1 Corinthians 13, his great chapter on love. Here is how Paul words this fundamental principle of growth and maturity: "When I was a child, I spoke like a child, I thought like a child, I reasoned like a child. When I became a man, I gave up childish ways" (v. 11). In becoming adults, we grow not just physically, but emotionally and spiritually as well.

One aspect of our growth is relating to our parents in a more mature way. This means that we can't keep being dependent on them in the same ways we once were. We need to take on more and more practical and emotional responsibility.

As an example, if your parents are financially supporting you, you need to actively work to relieve them of this responsibility as soon as possible. Doing this removes awkward confusion in the relationship between you and your parents about who bears financial responsibility in your life. If your parents are covering many of your major expenses after you marry, their investment often leads them to feel like they have the right to exercise accountability (and they might in certain circumstances), which can lead to conflict and will confuse loyalties, impeding your process of leaving and cleaving.

So while your parents may offer to help you financially in the early days of your marriage, when it comes time to replace a car that your parents bought for you when you were in high school, it really should be your responsibility. And if you can't quite afford it yet, it may be better to wait rather than to ask your parents to finance that purchase, simply because of the awkward pressure it introduces into the relationship.

When our daughter got married, her bank accounts were still visible to us. But she and her husband rightly discerned that our ability to see their finances could tempt us to editorialize on their financial decisions. So she and her husband made a wise decision to end our ability to view these accounts, removing any temptation my wife and I might have had to undermine our relationship.

The maturing process also means that as we take on more responsibility in our own lives, our view of our parents grows and changes. For instance, when we were young, we may have concluded that our mom or dad was neglecting us if they had to work late. In our youthful immaturity we may have allowed this idea to fester in our imagination, causing a rift between us and our parents. But now, as adults, we may also find ourselves in situations when we have to work late, which can help us understand that work time is often an issue out of our control, even if our spouse is at home waiting for us. Such newfound awareness may provide the opportunity to heal old wounds with our parents.

Thinking more maturely about relational disappointments in our past gives us a platform for more mature engagement with our parents as we move further into adulthood.

3. Move from self-centeredness to concern for others

Finally—and this may be the most important tool we place in our toolbox—God's Word teaches us to show concern for others. Up to the point of becoming adults, we've basically spent our whole lives being self-centered, thinking foremost about our own preferences, plans, and needs. As we age, we learn, little by little, to consider the needs and circumstances of the people around us. This process is accelerated when we get engaged and marry. Because of love, we are compelled to enter into the world of our spouse in order to empathize with their experiences and perspectives. We also learn to live with consideration of their schedule, needs, and desires. In these ways, God uses marriage to help us grow in Christlike care for others.

As we grow not only in maturity but also in our walk with the Lord, we see the outworking of the gospel in our lives. The Spirit strengthens us to show compassion, kindness, and humility (Colossians 3:12) and enables us to live out "the Golden Rule" (Luke 6:31). All of this increases our compassionate awareness of our parents and their life situation.

Practically, this means that if we want to plan a family outing with our parents, instead of deciding all the details and then inviting them in, we might do better to ask them what they would enjoy doing. Asking their preferences signals a humility and honor that considers their feelings and circumstances before our own.

Trying to get a clearer picture of the unique circumstances in our parents' lives may help us to understand some of the reasons why they may be pressuring us to do something different than we might want. For instance, if they are facing a looming college tuition bill for one of our siblings, they may be hesitant to agree to an expensive vacation and may counter our invitation with something much more affordable. Asking ourselves what we might do if we found ourselves in their position may present a redemptive opportunity for us to fulfill the biblical mandate to bear one another's burdens.

Proactive Strategies for Honoring Your Parents While Loving Your Spouse

Having looked briefly at some key biblical principles for establishing new yet loving parameters for our relationship with our parents, let's turn our attention to some strategies we might employ to honor them while loving our spouse.

Express your gratitude

One of the most profound gifts you can give your parents is expressing your gratitude for what they have done for you. This is because gratitude is the most practical and overt manifestation of honor. Expressions of gratitude are most poignant when they are done in thoughtful and specific ways.

Sending a note or card or having a conversation over the phone or in person will go a long way in encouraging them about the ways their love has made a difference in your life. It's the difference between a vague "Thanks for always being there for me" and specific gratitude: "Hey, Mom, do you remember that time I was deeply depressed when I broke up with my boyfriend? I've been thinking a lot about what you said to me that night, and I wanted you to know that not only your words, but also the time you took to just hug me while I cried was one of the most meaningful and important memories of my life. You are such a good listener, and you are full of such wisdom and grace. I am so thankful you are my mom!"

You can even take a sentiment like this and expand it into something more polished like a poem or a speech delivered at a birthday party or anniversary. Author Dennis Rainey refers to this as a *tribute*, which he defines as "A formal document or composition that publicly proclaims your gratitude for what your parents did right, for the positive qualities and values they passed on to you."[2]

However you show appreciation for your parents, your efforts will deeply enrich your relationship with them by giving them a sense of confidence about your love. This assurance will make it much easier for them to adjust to your leaving them and cleaving to your spouse.

Seek their counsel

Something I regularly hear from young married couples is that they wish their parents would stop offering them unsolicited advice. That makes perfect sense, but have you ever stopped to think about why parents tend to do this? It may arise from some flaw in them, but it may just as well come from the fact that they want to see you thrive and are eager to share their experiences with you. Their desire to be helpful doesn't always need to be perceived as intrusive.

To help prevent the tension that can arise from unsolicited advice, look for opportunities to seek your parents' counsel about a whole range of decisions. Giving them such an opening can be a powerful symbol of honor. It's also much easier on the relationship for you to offer information about your lives than for them to seek it out in ways that can feel intrusive. For instance, if you are considering something big like buying a house, consider asking your parents how they decided the time was right for their first home purchase. Initiating a conversation like this invites them into your lives but allows you to place some important limits on the conversation like, "We've heard some really interesting thoughts from a few of our friends but we want to get your insights on the pros and cons of buying versus renting before we settle the issue for ourselves." This will make your parents feel honored but also remind them they are not the ultimate decision makers.

It's important to recognize that your parents have already been through almost everything you are about to experience. Taking the time to seek their counsel every once in a while will alleviate some of the pressure they may feel to push in on you to offer it unsolicited, keeping the relationship in a much better place.

Propose opportunities to connect

Try to be proactive in offering opportunities to connect, especially around significant dates and holidays. Early in your marriage, reach out to both sets of parents to let them know that you are determined to cultivate a meaningful relationship with both of them. Express that one of the ways you want to do this is by working with them as early as possible to sort out details.

If you live near each other, get ahead of the curve by proposing some ideas for a regular time to connect for dinner. If you live in different areas of the country, take the time to anticipate any potential barriers that might impede your ability to get together with them over the holidays. In both situations make sure they know that even if you can't always be there with them on a specific day, you are going to do your best to find a satisfying alternative. Some couples have even settled on a consistent rotation of connection points (e.g., every other Sunday night at 7:00 p.m.) or holidays (e.g., every other Christmas) to relieve the tension of having this conversation year after year.

Keep the conversation open on the topics of spending time together and the need to make adjustments as life gets busier. This will send a clear signal of love and care for your parents, which will usually make them less rigid in their expectations of you.

Show them grace

Perhaps most meaningfully, keep the Bible's teaching about sin, repentance, and forgiveness at the forefront of your relational interaction with your parents. This is true whether they are Christians or not. They aren't perfect, and neither are you. As believers, we shouldn't have to strain to remember all the grace and mercy we've been shown by the Lord and fellow believers.

It's precisely these kinds of recollections that should inform the way we relate to everyone in our lives, especially our own family. Paul reminds us of this fundamental gospel principle in Colossians 3:12–13:

> Put on then, as God's chosen ones, holy and beloved, compassionate hearts, kindness, humility, meekness, and patience, bearing with one another and, if one has a complaint against another, forgiving each other; as the Lord has forgiven you, so you also must forgive.

The stresses of life, the pressures of work, and lingering feelings of relational angst can disrupt even the best of relationships, but the gospel gives us the tools to forgive and love even through seasons of pain.

When your parents hurt you, be the first to cover their sins. When you say something sinful or insensitive to your parents, be the first to express an apology. Remember, they've probably survived a lot of your immaturity and insensitivity over the previous years, so they can probably do it again!

Enter into conversations with this principle in mind, and it will help you not to become as rigid and defensive as you might be otherwise.

What If My Parents Aren't Responding?

If you've put these principles into practice but aren't having much success in overcoming relational difficulty between you and your parents, how should you proceed?

First, know you aren't alone. One of the most common counseling issues I deal with as a pastor is relational conflict between adult married children and their parents. Definitely seek the help of a pastor or biblical counselor when you face a serious breach of relationship with your parents. But before it reaches this point, you can also try these strategies for strengthening your relationship.

1. Seek the counsel of a trusted older Christian couple

Finding a couple or a person in your parents' generation or life situation can be a good place to start. These folks might come from your church or another ministry you are part of. Ask them to help you better understand what your parents might be thinking. Find out how they've navigated conflict with their own adult children and what important counsel they might have as you seek to establish better communication patterns.

2. Ask open-ended questions of your parents

If you can broach the topic of concern with your parents, then try asking them if it would be ok to dialogue about it in a more specific way. Instead of starting with your solutions, however, give them an opportunity to offer their own ideas about what might help to heal the rift you are facing.

Let's say the difficulty has to do with you being short with them because you are feeling pressured by them in some way. Start by telling them that you really do want to be able to discuss each other's lives but feel like the three of you haven't been communicating well. Ask if they have any ideas about how to improve the situation. While their answers might not be satisfying to you and your spouse, this gives you a framework to better understand where the differences lie. And if you can be respectful and listen well, they may be more likely to ask you to share some of your ideas about resolving the conflict.

3. Help them understand your situation

One of the most valuable tools for deepening understanding between you and your parents is making sure that they are aware (with your spouse's permission) of any special challenges in your life that may be indirectly impacting your relationship with them. Perhaps the reason you can't spend Christmas together this year is that your spouse is in a very precarious situation at work that will make taking extra time off very difficult. Or maybe you are waiting on the results of a medical test that has made you anxious, and you aren't mentally ready to schedule a vacation with them until the situation has been resolved.

One of the most challenging scenarios is if your spouse and your parents are not getting along. Although this can be very difficult to discuss, you may need to break the ice and talk about the issue, making your love and support of your spouse clear through the current season of conflict. If you find yourself in this situation, you can still affirm your love for your parents but may need to create some special boundaries to protect the long-term prospects of your relationship with them while still prioritizing your own marriage.

Conclusion

The holiday dilemma I described at the opening of this book was resolved by splitting our Christmas celebration between our two families. We spent Christmas Day and the days leading up to it with my wife's family and then boarded a plane to Florida on Christmas night to spend the following few days with my family.

It wasn't ideal for our families, and it wasn't ideal for us, but everyone made their best effort to bend a little while we tried to identify what each family needed from us at the time. In the case of my wife's family, it was meaningful to have our presence at a few key traditions with her extended family. In the case of my family, it was just as meaningful to get some quality time together directly after Christmas.

At the end of the day, marriage calls us to hold two commitments in balance: the biblical command to honor our parents and the covenantal call to love our spouse above all other people. That balance is rarely simple, but by moving from obedience to honor, from dependence to responsibility, and from self-centeredness to concern for others, we can cultivate marriages that are strong while still showing genuine gratitude, respect, and care for our parents.

Soli Deo Gloria!

Endnotes

1. *Strong's Exhaustive Concordance*, "3513. kabad or kabed," https://biblehub.com/hebrew/3513.htm.

2. Dennis Rainey and David Boehi, *The Best Gift You Can Ever Give Your Parents* (FamilyLife, 2004), ix.